A memoir written by

APRIL WILLIAMS

authorHOUSE®

AuthorHouse™ UK
1663 Liberty Drive
Bloomington, IN 47403 USA
www.authorhouse.co.uk
Phone: UK TFN: 0800 0148641 (Toll Free inside the UK)
*   UK Local: (02) 0369 56322 (+44 20 3695 6322 from outside the UK)*

Published by AuthorHouse   02/27/2023

ISBN: 979-8-8230-8118-4 (sc)
ISBN: 979-8-8230-8117-7 (e)

Print information available on the last page.

I dedicate this to my partner who has held my hand throughout my life's toughest hurdles and my first therapist, who saw me for more than what has happened to me.

Clip My Wings

As I try to fly

Further up the sky

My wings start to bleed

With angst and shame

It is with God I plead

I beg him to let me fly

But he says, "you do not belong in the sky"

I gradually get onto the ground

Where all I do is howl

I am where suffering lays

Can't seem to escape

Even when I pray

I am a magnificent bird

But all the people who believe what they heard

Clip my wings

They tell me that I belong on the ground

No story or sweet sounds

I am just what they make of me

One by one

Wing by wing

I become just like them

I can't seem to pretend

That I am happy here

They watch me frown

They love the product of my tears

I promise that I won't stay on the ground forever

They can't keep me with this tether

They can't shoot me down

I am bulletproof

Hurt me and you won't hear a sound

Let me fly

Into the sky

With full wings

No more cutting my hope

No more bringing me to your level

My wings are mine only

And you can't clip them without my say so

- Clip my wings

INTRODUCTION

During my university break I wanted to crack down on some gripping books. I intended to buy *I'm Glad My Mom Died* by Jennette McCurdy, but once I stepped foot into Waterstones on the 29th of December, I instantly was drawn to this personal novel – *When You Lose It,* by Roxy and Gay Longworth. Now, I should have known that the moment I picked that book up I was never going to be able to put it down. It was a book that I, and am sure many others, related to. Maybe it was a sign from the universe for me to pick up that book, because for the longest time I always felt misunderstood. Roxy and Gay simply put it into words just how daunting life can be on a young person and a mother too, which touched me. The raw emotions of the mother and daughter dynamic, the detail of how crippling mental health can be, and that's when I knew, that I had to write this book.

During this time of writing this book, I was still dealing with the hurdles that life was throwing at me. I was clinging onto dear life, wondering what my next steps were, despite having a thousand obstacles in my way. Nonetheless, sharing my story gave me hope. I have always been a writer, sharing my thoughts on a page. But never have I shared it with the world. Even though a lot of people doubted me on writing this book, the fact that I was connecting with hundreds if not thousands of readers gave me hope. Through my experiences, I've often felt lonely. The only thing that has gotten me through all the hurdles I've faced is that someone, anyone, will resonate with this story which would give them hope for a better future.

I decided to write about the things that I have healed from and come to terms with. I want to be able to write without reliving pain so that my perspective would be beneficial to readers, and also to myself. There are things that have been left out, and when I'm ready to discuss and share this with the world, I will be able to do this in a beautiful way.

Mental health is not easy to talk about, especially if you have suffered with it long term. The impact of generational trauma is often not talked about, and it is something I've never completely understood until recently. My family is a complicated one, something that I've never completely resonated with. From my mum's trauma to my father's, I began to battle with their pain as well as my own. At the end of 2022, I attempted suicide. I thought that would be it. That is me done with the world. But something tells me that I am not done. Something tells me that this book needed to be written, and I had to be the one to write it.

Throughout my life, I have immensely suffered with mental health issues – whether that be anxiety, depression, paranoia, insomnia, I suffered from it. I found that, during my adolescence, I couldn't begin to cope with these unbearable feelings I had inside of me, and I knew one day that it had to stop. I have read a lot of self-help books, trying to find out if these intelligent people with their experience in the psychological field could help me, but it was not as easy it I thought it would be. My life contained a lot of traumas, some unmasked to the point where it almost became unrecognizable. Reflection is a key part of this book, but sometimes reflecting on things that you don't understand can be incredibly frustrating. I look at my anxiety like a piece of string – it is long, jumbled, knotted. You take so long to unravel it, but when you touch it, your fingertips are on fire, burning memories that were vital to your part of discovery.

This thought-provoking memoir details every raw, sad and hopeful moments of my life. I hope this reaches whoever finds comfort in this book, just in the way I found comfort in Roxy and Gay's story. I have been very hesitant to write a book like this, it puts me at my most vulnerable. But I am done hiding my feelings. Every time I felt someone *clip my wings,* they took away my hope. This book allows me to look at my beautiful wings and welcome them to a new beginning. Because this a new start. For me and for you. So, thank you to everyone who has given me the courage to write this.

Part One

*A*t four years old, my parents split up. I couldn't even remember it properly, all I can remember is my dad always being there, but not my mum. She always worked, and for the longest time, this has affected me deeply. I only saw my dad on the weekends and in the holidays which was always something exciting to look forward to. But as I grew older, I needed him around a lot more, especially with the troubling relationship I grew to have with my mum.

Although this is my story, I would like to touch on my mother's. Her whole life has been about struggle. A Sierra Leonean immigrant first born daughter, coming to England by the age of seven with no family. No support. Nothing. She mentioned to me and brother about her notorious aunt who abused her as a child and hearing it in detail sent shivers down my spine. She then went into care at the age of fourteen, still in survival mode, not knowing any sort of normalcy like the rest of the world. I am telling you this because her background is an integral part of my journey, especially in the way my mum raised myself and my brother.

Throughout her life she has been alone, a single mother of two children, with nobody to hold her hand. My mother could only afford the necessities, and for that I will always be grateful. She worked hard to extensively take us on holidays, and it was magical. She truly was superwoman. But despite this, my mother faced battles that she had not yet dealt with, which had a huge impact on us as her children.

I have tried to pin down in words how the relationship with my mum affected me, but I don't think I can. I can only present to you the facts, alongside the intense emotions that came with it. Her presence or absence as I would say left a hole in my heart where my mother's love should have been. During primary school I became increasingly envious of my friends' relationship with their parents. This envy turned into resentment, and I soon began to hate my mum. I did never understand that instead of her being my parent, I had my brother that is four years older than me parenting me full time. We had the perfect relationship, me and my brother. There was never a moment that I hated the time we spent together. He would take to me to the parks on the weekend where we would play, he would teach me FIFA on his Xbox, and help me with my homework whenever I needed assistance. Although I loved this, I really wanted to have my mum around more. Because where was she? She worked all the time, and if she wasn't working, she was going on dates with men who never respected her. I hated that she did that to herself, partly because she never realised how precious her mind, soul and body was, and because they used her, they used us.

We had stepdaddies what seemed like every three to four months. They always thought they were some kind of authority figure to me and my brother, creating order around the house because we were 'too wild'. I hated all of them, and felt it was my mission to chase them away. My mother was not brave enough to tell and show these men that she deserved better, so I had to be the one to do it. This intensified the relationship between me and mother, and although I was trying my best to protect her, I began to hate her because she couldn't protect us from all the horrible things these men did to us. Although they were all terrible, there is one that stuck out from the rest. I won't name him because this is my story. Giving him a name gives him meaning. And I don't owe him that. He was the last boyfriend of mum's that I saw before I moved out at the age of twelve. He was also the last boyfriend of hers to ruin my perception of men which felt like forever. He had no job, no income. Just a charismatic charm that ironically my mother fell for. But I didn't. I could see through him, and he knew it. My mum adored him, he was everything she could have wanted. Someone to look after her kids. I just would like to add that my father was still in the picture at this point, but we did begin to see him less which I will touch on later. Before the situation began,

I despised my mum's boyfriend with my whole being. I couldn't imagine why, but I just did. I wanted my mum to step up at this point and take back control of the house instead of a stranger in my home telling me what to wear, eat or talk like.

As time passed, I began being more difficult with my mum and her boyfriend. I just wanted to scream from the top of my lungs for someone to save me from that awful home environment, because clearly my parents hadn't done a good job at that. She thought the best way of handling me was to beat me, but all it did was make me feel unloved, ashamed, and unworthy of real affection and time.

My stepfather said something to me that stuck with me for a long time. We had a heated moment; I can't even remember about what and I threatened to call my dad. He replied, "go on. If he will even answer. It's not like he will ever show up for you." And he was right. But that wasn't the point. When all of this was going on, where was my dad? I grew bitter over time and that turned into silence. Feeling unloved as a child is the most horrendous feeling to experience, and I won't ever forget that.

As I became quieter my mum's boyfriend became more controlling over me. We were left alone a lot, and I hated it. That is probably why I loved school as much as I did. It was my sanctuary. My safe place. One evening after school is a night I will never forget. I came in and tried to ignore him to the best of my ability. I didn't want any trouble and was so drained from fighting him all the time. So I had a shower, I love them. So refreshing. But when I came out, he was there. He was always there. Still ignoring him to my best ability, this time it didn't work. Maybe I should have said something. Maybe that would have made all the difference. He followed me into my room, took my towel off me and pinned me onto the bottom of the bunk bed. I was stricken with fear. I knew that no one was coming to save me. This time I wasn't silent. I said no. I said no a thousand times, and it still made no differences. He hunted me down as if I was his prey. He *clipped my wings* for the first and last time. It all happened so quickly that sometimes it feels like a dream. When it was over, my brother came back from school. At this point, my brother is in secondary school, roughly fifteen. I started to see him a lot less when my mum's boyfriend was there. He went down the stairs like nothing happened while I stayed in my room, still.

My household was never religious, but God was the only thing that kept me alive. I prayed to him almost every night, begging him to stop this misery called my life. He was like a figure of hope for me, and that is why after all the years he is the one I call upon, because he loves and knows me best. I wanted to be somewhere else, anywhere else; so I decided to run away. Although this wasn't the first time, the second time felt like it had more purpose. I was a wild child, no denying that. My mother thought she could tame me by beating me into submission, but it never worked. Instead, I became a rebellious child, refusing to let my mother beat me into fear. But although I kept my head held high, most days when she'd beat me began to put me further down the rabbit hole of numbing and darkness. The first time I ran away, I really wanted to be put into foster care. I didn't know much about the care system as I do now, but I knew that anywhere was better than home. It happened a second time because my first time obviously didn't work, and I had more of a plan. I would go further, bus to bus, train to train, and live on the streets. I never wanted to be in home with my mum or her boyfriend, and so I had to think more carefully. One day after school, I left. Doing exactly as I planned. But one flaw in my plan is the questions. It never even crossed my mind that a stranger may perceive me lost. One lady came up to me in the station of Bethnal Green and asked if I was homeless. I immediately said yes, even if I legitimately wasn't. Home was where the heart is, and my home was heartless. I walked with this lady and told her about my mum, but not about her boyfriend. I wish I did then. Maybe I wouldn't have endured so much suffering afterwards. Back then I was angry with the lady because she called the police who sent me home eventually, but now I understand. I am just mad at the child protection services who have no idea what children are going home to, and if their parents cannot keep them safe, they should at least try.

When it came home my mum locked me in a cage known as the home for a whole year. I wasn't allowed to leave the house apart from school or watch television or even go on school trips. This is where my anxiety started. I was intensely scared of my mum because of this which made me feel so numb inside. When she finally ungrounded me I started year seven. I was excited by the thought of interacting with new people and also going to the same school as my brother. But as beautiful as it sounds it wasn't always like that. I had freedom now yes, but I still felt like a prisoner. I never realised the impact of staying in that house for a whole year until now. It killed me. My ability to socialise with other people my age was hard. I pretended that my life was a fairytale, loving parents with good jobs. I sold the story to others and most importantly myself. I wanted to believe that all the bad things that happened to me did not happen. But this did not help me. I became angrier at my mother and other family members who decided to watch by. I don't think my mum understood what living with her at that time did to me. She just perceived me as the ungrateful, spoilt child who did not understand all the sacrifices she made for me. The truth is, I didn't know. All I knew was that she let bad things happen to me and did bad things to me, and that was not okay.

By the end of the school year, I was adamant on leaving my mum's house. I couldn't stand living with her and didn't even want to have anything to do with her. Luckily, my grandmother volunteered to raise me for as long as she could. I've always loved spending time with my grandma. She was sweet and we always did fun things together. When I moved in with her the first thing she did was decorate my room. It was pink and white with canvases saying 'live, love, laugh'. I guess

I needed to do those things since my life was becoming a comedy show with everyone watching in their front row seats. I started a new school and instantly made friends. This is ironic for me, especially because I have always found this part of life difficult. Even though I didn't need to try, I overtly tried extra hard for people to like me, often pretending to be someone I was not. I thought I learned the first time that this was not the answer. Clearly not. During this time my relationship with my mum really affected me worse than it did when I was living with her. I thought that I was free, but I still felt as if I was being silenced and ashamed about who I was. I always told the kids at school that I lived with my dad, and he was away on business making lots of money. It was better than to admit that I lived with my grandma because living with my mum was torture. I then met this boy at school who I'd never talk to in person, but we would talk to each other on social media. He called me beautiful and all sorts of things; I craved this sort of attention. We used to talk everyday after school on facetime, mainly because I was lonely being at home on my own. When you haven't had the right sort of attention in your childhood, consuming any sort of attention can be dangerous. I gave him explicit photos of me which were later exposed. My dad found out. He wasn't even mad at me. He said that he would always be proud of me, and sometimes I just wanted him to be mad. For him to care about my wellbeing enough to save and protect me from all the bad things.

My dad was and will always be a special part of my life. He made me the happiest in the best way he could, so I owe him that acknowledgement. When I was younger, he was very ill. He suffered from sickle cell, and although I was aware of it, my family tried to shield me from it the best they could. I can't remember much of how ill he got, just that he seemed to be spending more and more time in the hospital. He was due a liver transplant, but it is what seemed like forever. He was getting sicker over time, and I was always scared of losing him. He was the only person at that time that saw me for me than what I was, and always made me feel like I was someone to be proud of. So when he got sick, the joys of my childhood faded. I couldn't picture any happy memories. Before his liver transplant, there was little to no hope of him getting a transplant or even making it to the theatre. So he decided to make his last memories less gloom and doom by taking us on holiday to Saint Vincent. It was beautiful. The food. The sea. Everything. I can tell that he was very happy there. And so was I. I had never been to a place so mesmerising; I could smell the salt from the sea, I enjoyed the wind brushing on my face as it curved the palm trees and tasting the succulent food that made me feel closer to my culture more than ever. He took us on a yacht in Grenada to get to St. Vincent, where my brother got seasick and me and my elder cousin just watched as we saw the palm trees in the distance. My grandmother took me, my brother and my cousin to the sea when we arrived. It was the first time I saw a sea, but also one I'll never forget the image of due to a man killing a turtle in the sea, brimming its blood through the fluorescent colours of St. Vincent's finest view.

My father has always been an important part of my life and knowing that this was his happy space glistened me from the insides. He has always found passion in the smallest things, such as music which really stood for how joyous he is as a person. Even when we went to St. Vincent he D.J'd. I remember sulking because I wanted him all to myself, not away in the country performing for strangers who could never comprehend how special he was and is. Nonetheless, you could say that my father is a very eager man when it comes to travelling. He has always enjoyed the sights of life that only you can experience from the eyes. Being in Saint Vincent was a memory locked in our brains forever. I'll never forget that.

This acute happiness was short lived unfortunately. My auntie had a neighbour with a daughter the same age as me. We used to always play together. Little did I know how much that would change. When we got back from Saint Vincent my father and brother broke the news to me that she died. I still til this day don't know how. I refused to believe it. Little kids don't die at the age of six. They play outside and are just happy about life. Every time I went to my auntie's I always knocked for her, but her mum kept on telling me she is not here at the moment. I wish she told me the truth. Maybe then I would have believed it if it was coming from her. But deep down, I knew. After this moment I don't know what happened to me. Where my happiness went. All I knew was that there was a possibility that my father was going to die, and my best friend was already dead. The following year my dad got his transplant. I was so relieved. I was going to have my father for a longer time.

Despite this, me and my mum were going through a rough patch. Around the age of seven, I realised that she was not around as much, and it changed me. I started to display what some would call behavioural issues. At the time, I couldn't even comprehend what was going through my brain – but as I grew older, my behaviour was directed at my mum, and I just couldn't understand why. All I knew is that I began to despise her, and that was enough for me to stop wanting to behave like a normal child. The age of seven was a long time ago for me, so I am not going to pretend that I remember everything I knew then, but what I can tell you is that when we moved house, it was a huge turning point for me. From loving everything I knew in Walthamstow, to now living in the streets of crime of Leyton, I hated it. I never knew my mum's situation back then, but what I felt as a child growing up in an unsafe place felt even more important.

I started a new school, just across the street from the block of flats I lived in. This was the first time I was perceived as the new girl. At first, it wasn't so bad. I made a few friends who were nice and had loving parents, but for some reason they had everything I wanted, so I began to hate my life from this point on. I made a particular friend who eventually moved into the block of flats where I lived. She became the new girl after me, and in short, she wasn't very nice. A lot of the people did not like her, but they had good reason to. Despite this, I still liked her. Probably because she was similar in ways that nobody else could see but me. We eventually became the best of friends, coming to one another's homes practically everyday to baking with each other. But the more she came over to mine, the more she belittled me for having less than her. And I had a lot less. She told everybody at school that my mum only bought me a One Direction lamp for Christmas, which was true, but I didn't want to be pitied by the kids who had parents with a feasible amount of income; enough to buy more than a lamp for Christmas. My friend and I stopped talking after that. I didn't want to trust anybody from that point onwards.

I so desperately wanted my old life back; living in the one-bedroom flat in Walthamstow where everything and everyone was an integral part of my happiness. I told my mum that I wasn't happy here, but my life at that moment was set in stone. This is the moment my behaviour became radicalised, and although it led to everything that came afterwards, I wished I would have distinctively told somebody I was struggling. Sometimes, children find it hard to express their emotions in a healthy way, and amicably it should be the parent's role to spot that something is wrong. But my mum never did. She just saw me as a troubled child. So a troubled child I became. School became my route of escapism, somewhere that I could pretend that my life was a bed full of roses, but deep down it wasn't. The only happy part of my life at that moment was that I had my brother, and he was all I had. How unfair is that.

Part Two

*A*fter my father got better, he introduced us to a new lady. She was a divorcee with two sons and a daughter. It was fun spending time with them – I was so excited to have a new extended family. My father played house with his new partner and her kids, and it often struck me that he never wanted to have that family life with me or my brother. We still got to see him on weekends, which was always thrilling because we'd get to do cool, irrelevant things that children enjoy.

Later, my brother and I started to stay around there's more. My dad has had girlfriends in the past but nothing serious like this one. He was "in love" – something that I had never seen before. My mother of course, envied this. We spent more time with them than her, and I guess you could say that she was hurt. I never understood this, mainly because growing up my mother never really put in the effort to spend time with us, and because someone was doing her job at a much better rate, she felt undermined. An impact of having immense family/ generational trauma is that your brain fades the happy memories away. I distinctively cannot remember the happier times in my life, and that brings me great sadness. But what I can tell you are the tragic moments that became definitive, and how I am trying to heal from that. Part-time living with my dad's new family was a blessing and a curse. It meant that I didn't have to see my mum as much, but also the tremendous things that happened there that I kept quiet for so many years. I got along with everyone in the house; we'd hang out together and play outside whenever we could. I also spent a lot of time with my dad's girlfriend cooking, watching her and her daughter do their hair and makeup. The girly things that I wished I had with my mum but was lucky enough to witness about it then.

Soon, however, this would change. Everywhere I spent with family I began to resent. Especially where my dad was living. Me, my brother, and her two sons all used to share beds together in one medium sized room. You could probably imagine

24

how uncomfortable that must feel. But that wasn't even the worst of it. The youngest son of my dad's girlfriend took a liken to me in a peculiar way. At night, he used to touch me. I never told anyone because I never truly understood it. At a young age the sexual feelings that one might feel could be disguised as them discovering themselves in a sexual way. Nonetheless, that doesn't make any of it right. It began to happen too frequently, especially when I was sleeping, and I hated the way that made me feel. I never told my dad about this for many reasons: he was happy with the family situation that we were in and I thought that he would never believe me. I was a young girl who was very muddled, and lost innocence at an incredibly young age.

In addition, I started to not like the relationship that I had with my dad's partner. In many ways I began to treat her like my mum, as I found her to be ruthless in her ways. Sometimes her and my dad would fight and argue, and I didn't appreciate it because this environment began to feel very much like my mum's. His partner and him revealed the news to us that she was pregnant. Deep down I already knew this. I love children, and the fact that she was giving me a little brother or sister was a dream come true. In June of 2013, my little sister was born. I was the happiest sibling alive. I no longer was the youngest child and I had someone to care for and love. But unfortunately, it didn't turn out this way. I began to be quite envious of my little sister due to the love my dad gave her. I wondered why he didn't love me and brother like that, so I became bitter and angry. Although I had been blind to it as a child, every time my father has a child with someone new he gives the newborn everything that he didn't give the previous child/children. My father has two older children than me who he doesn't see, and they stayed away for plenty of good reason.

My father is what you would call a serial adulterer. His first mother to his two children was young when she met my dad, and what some might call naïve. He was unfaithful to her with my mother and did not make as much time and effort to see his children as he should have. As a result, the relationship that I have with my older sisters has always been strained from the start, mainly because the time that my dad spent with me, he should have also spent with them as well. Despite this, when I was younger, I did see them from time to time. I used to go over to their mum's flat and make cupcakes with them. They even brought me to Butlins in 2011, which was the last time I saw them before I became estranged with my parents[1]. During a time when I was not seeing my dad as frequently, he told me that they had a massive fallout that led him no contact rights by law. I was thinking that what he did must have been really terrible, and it was. I am not going to detail what he did, mainly because that is their story to tell, but only that he had a physical altercation with my oldest sister in front of my other sister, which in itself is frightening to experience and

---

[1] I went into care when I was fourteen when I was not in touch with my father and pursued contact with them.

witness. When he told me, I was devastated. Mainly because I never knew that the man that I have adored my whole life would be capable of such a thing and also because the memories with my sisters had come to an end. I also decided that in the moment, I would forgive him. He was the only person that stuck by me, and I believe that people deserve second chances.

So when my little sister was born, I wanted to be as present as I could. Despite all the issues and the jealousy, I didn't want history to repeat itself. This was short-lived though, as you could probably imagine. I stopped seeing my dad after a while because my relationship with him began to change too. I saw him for the dishonest man he was, and perhaps he didn't like that so much. I remember that for a brief time, he started to see my mum again romantically. Of course I was happy, having both loving parents like the fairytale that I wanted. However, it also made no sense that he would be with her if he was raising a child with the last mother of his child and her family. I ignored this, as some might say, ignorance is bliss. But it isn't. Facing up to the truth has more power than anything and I never wanted to turn out just like my parents had – dishonest and hurtful.

This romance was short lived, and I was back to the devastating relationship with my mother. As I mentioned in *Part One*, I went to live with my grandmother. The realisation that your family is not normal, and that you did not have average parents hit you hard. It certainly did me. Although I love my grandma, I did not want to live with her. There is a certain relationship you have with your grandparents – a certain distant one, and I could not maintain that type of relationship living with her. She worked Monday to Friday, in a nursery, and she absolutely loved her job. But I didn't get to see enough of her, which was not good for my emotional development at the time.

The new school I started involved pertaining to a different type of personality. I found that I could adjust to environments where I felt anxious, in order to fit in. I did everything I could to do that, whether it was changing my hairstyle or to having a new boyfriend every month, I did it. Soon, I would later find out that I was labelled as a slut, which began to brand me in ways that I never expected. Anytime anyone would ever talk about me, that is what they thought. Not that I was smart, or funny, or just good company. Just a slut. I hated being perceived that way, as most schoolgirls do, mostly because I could not control the narrative. And that is when my self harm journey began[2]. It was towards the end of year eight that I began to cut myself all over my arms. Something about doing that to myself felt soothing to me, despite hating the feeling of all kinds of pain. I hid it from everyone for a long time. I'd start small, but later found it to be an addiction. I was scared to tell my family that I was struggling due to the fact I didn't want to be seen as an attention seeker and also because no one in my family had ever spoken about these sorts of things with our relatives. I

---

[2] I had self-harmed from the ages of thirteen to eighteen, which will be explored.

constantly listened to sad music, whilst cutting, and it was taking a toll on me. During this time, my ability to socialise became less and less, and certain pupils in my academic year began to dislike me. I had an argument with a girl who told me that my act was all a façade, that I wasn't actually brave like I pretended to be. She saw me for who I was, and that frightened me.

That was the moment I attempted my first suicide. I got a pack of pain relief and I consumed all of them in the night. When I woke up in the morning, I was shocked that I hadn't died. Disappointed. My grandmother told me I was going to be late for school, so I got dressed, left the house, but didn't go to school. I had been skipping school a few days prior because I was scared that people at school were going to try and hurt me, and I so badly did not want that to be the case. I had rather hurt myself than give anyone the power of hurting me instead. The next day of my attempted suicide, I walked around the area in which I lived in at the time. I was scared, I didn't know what to do. I didn't understand why I wasn't dead, because I so desperately wanted to be. But now I have a feeling I was never supposed to die, and deep down I have always known that. So, I did the one thing that I never thought I'd do at that moment. I called ChildLine. They sent me out an ambulance quite quickly and were really nice and understanding. I needed that. But it wasn't until I got to the hospital that everything started to fall apart. I was asked questions by the doctor, and I didn't want to relive the decision I had made prior to coming here. First, my grandmother arrived. She was livid. She thought I was selfish for what I had done, especially because she had a heart problem at the time. I consumed her words because that's exactly how I felt. Selfish.

After that my father came, and the way he looked at me as if someone had shot his heart and the blood flew down the drain. That look haunted me. I felt a wave of sadness and regret because I didn't think about what this would do to my family. Shortly after, my mother arrived. I couldn't face her.

I didn't want to. So, I left my hospital bed, and told her to leave as I was going to the bathroom. When I came back the nurses told me that she was crying. The thing is, suicide is never easy on families. It can be what rips them apart. I never intended it to be a moment where my family suffered from great loss and tragedy, but all I knew in that moment was that my sadness was too painful to live with. During this time I saw a mental health nurse, who was trying to understand why I did what I did. There were some things that I refrained from telling, such as the domino effect of my family dynamic. One question he asked me was why I called ChildLine. I don't know. I never really knew. The more I think about it the more I just wanted to scream about the pain I was in, begging someone to help me. Maybe this was the beginning for my new journey of speaking my truth.

During the duration of my stay, I spoke with social services. They proposed that I could stay in a temporary foster home while things die down in my family. Of course, my dad was against this, mainly because my grandmother was in care and her experiences weren't the nicest. So as I stayed there for a couple of days, my dad was conjuring a solution. That I would come to live with him. I had hope again. I could start afresh. See my sisters grow up[3]. Start a new school and try to make friends. Yeah, I could see that happening. And it did, for the most part. When I initially moved in I had a long talk with my dad's partner. I immediately felt vulnerable because I had all these feelings conjured up inside and now, I had to be honest and let them out. I was ready for a new beginning, even if I didn't know what that would look like. I was just hoping that the pain wouldn't feel so unbearable anymore.

After a couple of months of being out of school, I had finally been accepted to attend a school that my stepbrother attended. I was happy for a fresh start, and to make new friends with my dad by side. But little did I know that it required more

---

[3] My dad's partner had another daughter

than a dream for this to be true. I was the new girl for the third time in my life, and I guess you could say that I was done trying. I didn't make the effort to make new friends, thus, I was perceived as unapproachable. I thought this move was going to be a lot different, but the feelings of pain and suffering in silence still stayed the same. The only people I really knew was my stepbrother's friends and a friend from my English class. She was awkward, like me, and that is why I probably took a liking to her. She was sweet yet sheltered. Life had thrown some hurdles at her, thus the reason for keeping in her shell. When we became friends, she was the only person I felt to trust. My gut instinct told me that I could find a friend in her forever, and that is true til this day. We used to spend a lot of time together in the pastoral office, mainly because she was anxious to be around people and that I was struggling with my own demons. Although the "popular" kids grilled me for hanging around someone like that, I didn't care. On this planet, she was the only person who saw me, despite my mistakes and trauma. And for that, I am eternally grateful. We never hung out outside of school, mainly because my dad and his partner didn't let me go outside on the weekends if I wasn't with them. I didn't really care though, I was just happy to see her when I could.

In March of 2018, I never knew that I wouldn't see her for years. The fairytale of living with my dad was coming to an end. He was spending quite a lot of time in the hospital, so I saw him a lot less during this time. One night in the February half term[4], an event happened that changed my life forever. I was sleeping in the room with my stepbrother and four-year-old sister at the time. I felt someone's fingers tracing my skin, and it immediately felt like I was in danger. I have been through this before, men thinking they have autonomy over my body, and that is exactly what was happening. I opened my eyes, and he was penetrating me with his fingers. I immediately

---

[4] A couple of days after my fourteenth birthday

panicked, lost for words. I often looked back and wondered why I didn't say anything. All I knew was that I couldn't believe that this was happening to me again. The day after, I didn't speak to anyone, especially not him. All I wanted to do was to run away. After all, it's the only thing I know. And eventually I did.

After the incident, I ignored my dad's partner for a whole week. I just couldn't look at her without seeing him; the monster she created. She caught on and took it out on my dad. We were kicked out briefly. We spent the week at my aunt's, and we talked. We talked about what my stepdad did to me and how he said that he would never let anyone do that to me again. But it was too late. Someone already did. Someone he brought into my life. And that is when I knew that I was the only one to protect myself from here on out. While I was still at my aunt's house, he went back home to talk to his partner. They figured things out and I immediately felt a wave of panic. I didn't want to go back there, yet I knew I had no choice. When I got back all three of us talked. They all blamed me for my behaviour, naming me selfish and horrible. They wanted to know what was really going on, but I couldn't say a word. This time, I clipped my own wings. That is when I decided that I would leave the next day, with no suspicion.

The next morning, I left like normal. Pretended to make my way to school, with the intention of leaving. I sat in a café in the town where we lived, just watching cars going by. I imagined that I would run into one and my life would be over, and I'd be content. But of course, I would also be ruining the driver's life too. So I sat in the café for hours on end, watching people as they ordered their coffees and left eventually, until I decided to leave. A couple of months prior, I attempted my second suicide. I was sent to a rundown hospital, which really wasn't a hospital. The nurses were lovely, and they had given me inspirational talks about how they have moved past their pain to create something beautiful with their lives. But I couldn't. Not then anyway. I was lost of all hope but knowing that these nurses understood somewhat of my pain, gave me a glimmer of hope. When I ran away, I went to see the nurse that treated me. She wasn't on shift, but she came straight away when she heard that I was looking for her. We sat and talked, and then finally I told her what happened to me. It felt like a burden and a relief at the same time because I knew what needed to happen next. The police.

The police came and I told them what happened, just as I told her, and then I had to make a formal statement in the police station. This meant that everybody in the house would find out about what happened. I felt panicked. Scared. What would my dad think? Will he believe me? Will he stay by my side? He didn't. And that is when I knew that I lost everything. He told the police officer who was dealing with my case that he didn't want me to come back. I lost everything in a heartbeat. The police called my stepbrother in for questioning, and he denied everything. My dad's partner supported him with this, branding me as a liar. I felt trapped in a circle of nothingness. All I could do was cry. For once, I didn't want to feel silenced, and by speaking my truth, I had every cost to pay. The only next solution that the police offered me was to stay with my mum, the woman I'd been trying to escape for many years. We drove all the way into London, where my mum was living. The police called and called, knocked and knocked, but no answer. She turned her back on me. Again. I had no idea what to think, only that I had nobody, and my life was truly ruined. The last solution that they gave me - the care system.

Part Three

I stayed in emergency care for an estimated month. I was assigned a social worker who listened to my story. He cried. I wanted to tell him that my pain isn't all that bad, but it was. It was horrendous, and there was no way of escaping it. Where I stayed was nice, the house was practically a detached mansion, I had my own room with a tv, and I spent most of my time thinking. Although the situation at hand was not ideal, I was glad that I got out. My peace of mind had long been a sacrifice, and now I was free. My parents tried to get back into contact with me, but I denied. They don't get to repair what they broke only because I'm in the care system, a file, with another sad story to tell.

I started to accept that this was my life from now on. I didn't know where I would go from there but as long as I was safe that is all that matters. I still felt haunted by my stepbrother and what he could possibly do to me if he found out where I was. I started to have nightmares, reliving every detail. It felt so real to the point I'd be screaming in my sleep. I may have been free, but my mind was a prisoner. While I was in the emergency home, I met this girl who I believe was sixteen at the time. The host labelled her as a troubled girl and warned me to stay away. When I met her, she was lovely. This is when I knew that the people who take care of us don't understand our experiences, and only see us for the trauma. She had been through some awful things, but none of that mattered to me. She was beautiful inside and out. She was crazy too, no denying that, but she carried herself well. Since I didn't have a phone, and she was the only one who did, we'd use her phone together. She had an app where you could talk to people online, and I found this particularly strange. She seemed to enjoy it, talking to older men who prayed on younger girls. Although I necessarily didn't like it, I still stayed with her while we did those things. The host that we lived with found out, and needless to say, she wasn't happy about it. She warned me about how troubled she was and thought her influence could send me down a dark path because I seemed impressionable. But I didn't care. She was my friend, and I was in no position to judge her. I often wonder about the people that I met along the way who have contributed to the person I am today. I think I wouldn't be anything without these experiences.

Finally, I moved out of emergency care and lived in a temporary foster home. It was just me, the foster carer and her daughter. It was lonely. She watched me like a hawk, which often made me feel like a prisoner. I wasn't allowed to be on my own without her supervision, and deep down I wanted to be. I wanted to be alone. Being around people didn't make me feel less lonely. When I stayed with her, she gave me pocket money. It felt so weird to be told that this money was mine, and I could spend it weekly. My parents never really gave me money, so this felt like a sort of privilege. She took me to one of the big shopping malls in her town, where we went to Primark. I brought some essentials, and a diary where I could write my poetry. Poetry was my only form

45

of expression; I find writing your words on paper was better than saying them out loud. After all, nobody could judge you if they don't know what you've written, especially if the words are for you and you only. The police visited me whilst I stayed there, asking me more questions about the situation with my stepbrother. This meant that I was going to have to do a follow up interview to confirm everything that I revealed when I gave my initial statement. Reliving those memories for the second time was really hard for me because I wanted to forget about what happened. When I went for the interview, I told them again, but this time I felt more sad about it. I was in the care system because I ran away and told the police what happened, and so I couldn't help but blame myself. They said they would follow up with me to let me know the progress of the case, and that was it for now.

Eventually I left my temporary foster home, into a more permanent foster home, which I was glad of. The foster parents were in their sixties, very religious, and of African descent. They were nice at first but the more I think about it, the more I think that they tried to shape me in their own image. I was still my own person and being without family meant that I needed to navigate my own way through life. I met their family and people that they knew from the church they attended but it felt all surreal. I joined their church for a while but felt overwhelmed at the feeling of confessing my love for God. My relationship was personal, and I didn't feel comfortable sharing that with a bunch of strangers.

Shortly after, I started a new school, which was chosen by the social services. The school wasn't all that great, but it did have good effects on me. At the start of the school year, I didn't really take it seriously. I just made new friends and I was still adjusting to the new situation. I wanted to fit in and pretend that once again, my life wasn't the way it was. I told the people at my school that I lived with my grandparents, and that was it. Being in care meant that once a month I had

47

to go to meetings known as 'Pupil's Education Plan' and 'Child in Care Review' to discuss my education and also my progress in general. My grades took a slam dunk due to the instability of moving around too many schools. I had no hope for my education at this point, only that I could survive through this chapter. Nonetheless, social services and the school were determined to help me, and I couldn't have been more grateful. Things that should matter began to matter, and that made me extremely happy.

My home life with my new foster family was becoming difficult. I was struggling a lot with my mental health, and that's not something that they understood. I had an assessment at CAMHS[5] where I told them about all of the things that happened to me. Initially I didn't get the reaction that I was expecting. They thought I was fine, but I wasn't. I knew that. I had just suffered an ordeal, still begging for help. My foster mother even told

---

[5] Children and Adolescence Mental Health Service

them that I was fine, happy even. Even when she knew I was not. I was angry and upset at the fact that the children's service let me down, and also the fact that my foster mother was so blind to the fact I was in a lot of pain. I decided that at that moment, my thoughts and feelings will no longer be vocalised, because nobody was listening.

After a year of being with my new foster family, I still wasn't happy. It was becoming more and more difficult within the household, in addition to my relapse of self harming. I was cutting again, this time on my inner arm. I felt weak and ashamed because this meant that I was no longer in control of what was happening to me. I accidently left out the razor blades in my bedroom, leaving my foster parents to find out. I felt a sudden wave of panic, then anger. I felt that my privacy was invaded, but realistically they had every right to check up on me. My foster mother immediately called the out of hours services, telling them I self-harmed to stray away from the attention of her fortieth anniversary. That hurt. I would have been able to tell her sooner if she didn't act like mental health was a forbidden disease that anybody could discuss. She truly believed that depression came from the devil, so that meant that I was doomed to hell.

While they were downstairs in the living room, I escaped through my bedroom window, running as fast as I could. I called my friend from school and asked if I could stay with her for a few days, and she said yes. She lived with her dad, two sisters, and her stepmother. Her dad asked if my foster parents knew I was here, and I immediately said yes. I didn't want to tell him that they didn't know where I was because I knew I would have to go home, and I really didn't want to. What seemed like a few days turned into a week, as my social worker found out where I was and I told her that I didn't want to go back there, which meant she had to find me somewhere else to stay.

My social worker found me somewhere to stay. She told me that we were a perfect match. I often thought she said that because the foster carer was black, but actually we were a perfect match based on personality. As we drove half an hour to the foster carers' home, I began to feel anxious. I didn't want to meet a new family and have the same experiences like the last one. I had no choice but to suck it up and say hello to this new family. When we arrived she greeted us at the door, she looked like she was in her mid forties, had blue and black braids, with a small dog I could hear in the background. Her house was big, with seven rooms and an outside pool with the longest garden I had ever seen. Firstly, she talked to my social worker on her own whilst I was outside in the garden. Her dog looked old, a mixed breed of a Yorkshire Terrier and Jack Russel. She was fast, with her petite legs and was very loud despite the size of her. Although I am more of a cat person, I took a liken to this dog. It was a family dog, so I treated the dog as such. They called me back in to discuss the plan. I was to stay there for a few weeks until I could find somewhere more permanent to stay. Shortly after my social worker left, the foster carer introduced me to the rest of the household. I first met her mother who had her own annex within the house. She said that I reminded her of her granddaughter – she was right because we look like a split image of one another. I met her other foster children, one older boy and then two siblings who were three years apart. The girl was quite rebellious in nature; she never wanted to be in the house, had a secret phone as we weren't allowed to have our phones overnight, and was suspected of doing drugs. Her brother was less quiet. He enjoyed spending time in the home, but sometimes it became too much for the foster carers because he had ADHD which exacerbated his anger issues. I didn't seem to quite mind his behaviour, he was the first person that I was initially close to in the house as we spent quite a lot of time together. The oldest foster child was an asylum seeker. He didn't speak much English, but his efforts to learn allowed him to achieve lots of awards for his hard work and dedication at his college. I later met my other foster carer who worked as a lorry driver part-time, and the other time looking after the child who had ADHD. He was funny, never serious, but he was the kindest man I ever met. Later in the evening, I met the foster carer's children. They were both in their twenties, one as a software engineer and the other as an IT analyst with a young daughter. Although the house was chaotic at times due to the dynamic of the household, I really enjoyed staying there.

What was supposed to be weeks, turned into a permanent placement. I didn't want to leave as I settled very quickly and had adjusted to this new family. My foster mother would drive me to school and pick me up afterwards. She began to dislike this though, as I could never get a bus because she lived in the middle of nowhere. Once I went back to school after the easter holidays, I had an emergency Child in Care Review. It was to plan out my placement to think of the possibility of a permanency, which is kind of like adoption. I was happy about this because I felt that there was somewhere I finally belonged. We also talked about the option of me starting a talking therapy so I could work through the things that I experienced, and I agreed to that. I finally felt after a long time that somebody was listening, and now I was visible.

I had an assessment review at CAMHS to discuss what type of therapy I would have. I was anxious because once again, I had to relive the traumatic events of my past. They diagnosed me with severe anxiety, mild depression, and panic disorder on the basis of childhood trauma. It was written in stone, the trauma. I didn't want to have these labels and just wanted to shut everyone away. Despite this, I was happy to finally be getting some help, what seemed like a long time. I was still self-harming after I left my previous placement as I began immensely depressed. I had buried a lot of things, mostly because facing them would mean I had to be put in a vulnerable position, and I didn't want that. I also was struggling with sleep a lot, having strong nightmares that would wake me up in cold sweats. Waking up the next day for school was hell because I barely would have slept the night before, and so my attention at school was side-tracked because I just wanted to sleep. At the start of year eleven, I was finally on the waiting list for therapy and started to receive Cognitive Behavioural Therapy. I had to learn coping mechanisms when I felt stressed or panicked. It was quite useful talking to someone, but that didn't change the fact that I was still struggling and would be struggling for years.

In the summer, at the end of year ten, my foster parents took me and everyone else on holiday. We went to Italy, and I was so excited! I loved the city Rome, and the ice cream (you could literally find ice cream shops everywhere in Italy) was so delicious. We stayed in an apartment complex in Anzio, which was quite close to Rome. We were given pocket money to spend whilst we were in Italy, so I bought a couple of souvenirs to remember the trip. I bought a key chain, and a purple bracelet. Purple has always been my favourite colour, so I thought that the bracelet was practically made for me. My foster dad brought a new t-shirt because he spilt chocolate ice cream over the one he wore. When we went to Rome, we walked for hours just exploring the city, and it was nice. All of our phones had died so we didn't take many photos, but this moment was only something that could only be recollected through memory.

There was a beach that took a five-minute walk; the view was mesmerising to say the least. This was the first time I had worn a bikini anywhere, and showing my body made me feel quite nervous. Nonetheless, I let the sun glisten on my skin and smell the sea near the sand. It kind of reminded me of when I went to St. Vincent, only that I was with different people, who had no intention of hurting me. Me, my foster brother and foster sister went on a canoe; we were quite far away from the shore, and unexpectedly, we were under water. This is when I realised that I couldn't swim that well, or at all. I thought I was going to die. My foster sister got me to shore, but she was mad because I held onto her whilst trying to get closer, which was hard for her as she was only small and also struggling under the water. I would never forget that day; mainly because it was traumatic but also because I felt it was an experience that one cannot forget. When we went back to the apartment complex, I was grilled for it. I felt humiliated and embarrassed, I just wanted to have fun like the others, but I just kept quiet and apologised. We went out later that day and I was still sulking, so my foster mother snapped. It triggered me a little, but I had to remember that we are on a holiday together, so a tantrum is not what is needed.

During this time, I was talking to a boy online. This is the first time I had talked to anyone romantically, especially after all that has happened to me. He lived quite far away from where I was living, so we talked on the phone all the time. He was also on holiday himself, which was nice because then we could tell each other all about it when we would finally meet. I told my foster carer that I would like to meet him once we are back in England. She was hesitant at first, mainly because I was only fifteen going to meet a stranger, but she finally agreed after we talked about a safety plan. We agreed to meet in London and have dinner together and really get to know each other personally. When we met, I was nervous. This was the first time in years that I have travelled to London on my own. It took me roughly an hour to get to London Charing Cross, as this was halfway for the both of us. We went to a park and sat and talked for ages. It felt natural, and so I no longer felt nervous. I really liked him, and I couldn't get to know him more than I did.

The next day, I started school. I was in my final year in secondary school, so this meant that I had to work extra hard this year. I had been staying with my foster parents for five months now, so I was settled now enough to focus on my GCSEs. I was behind quite a lot, so I decided that I would do extra work after school with my maths teacher. Maths has never been my subject; I like something that challenges me and where I can prove my point. But nonetheless I knew that I needed to pass maths, and so I worked really hard at it. I had a new maths teacher in the final year who changed my life. She was kind and inspired me to follow my dreams. I hadn't even thought about my life after I went into care but knowing that she believed me made me feel like I could. Every day after school, I'd stay with her and study. She'd even help me with other subjects that were non-maths related, and I was so grateful. My grades were eventually going up, and without her help I probably wouldn't have passed. I also was given a maths tutor who would come to my house once a week, where we'd do past papers for two hours. I was incredibly determined to pass, as I wanted all my struggles to count for something.

At the start of the year, I started to look around local sixth forms. I liked the look of two, but one stuck out to me. It was closer to where I lived, half an hour by bus. It was a Christian sixth form who pursued their students' academia to the fullest.

I wanted to be like the sixth form students that presented at the open day and knew that I was going to work my hardest to do that. I made my application on the portal that night, applying to study English Literature, Sociology, History, and Philosophy and Theology, alongside an Extended Project Qualification[6]. I know, this sounds like a lot. But I had never had this much hope and ambition with my education before, but I always knew that the doors that it was going to open could be endless. The other sixth form was an all-girls school, in an area that was about forty-five minutes from where I lived. I would have had to take different A-levels because of the limited selection. Although I liked their ethos of women empowerment, I didn't want to choose A-levels where my heart wouldn't be totally in it. Nonetheless, I still applied so that I would have a backup plan, choosing English Literature, Health and Social Care, and Business studies. I was

---

[6] EPQ is worth 28 UCAS points and most universities lower a grade if you have achieved an A or higher in this.

already taking Business Studies as a BTEC and found it quite enjoyable and interesting. I chose health and social care as my backup plan of becoming a mental health nurse, but this wasn't a career I had my heart in pursuing. The boy I was talking to was also looking at sixth forms, and it was nice that we were sharing that experience.

I saw him every other weekend for a while and met his parents. They were nice, and very fancy. They sent him to a boarding school, so he was only there on weekends, but had dropped out after he tried to kill himself. He then started to attend a state school, which he found was less challenging but easier on his mental health. He talked to me about sex, and that made my throat feel like it had barbed wire in it. I didn't want to have sex for so many reasons, but mainly because of my past that I hadn't gotten over at that time. He said to me that it is what people do when they are in love, so if I loved him, I would have sex with him. So I did. I didn't feel present, but he enjoyed himself, so I guess I was happy that he liked it. When I went home, I cried in silence. I never wanted to see or talk to him again, so I didn't. I never wanted to hurt him or make it seem like it was his fault, but I wasn't ready and he shouldn't have put that on me. When we last spoke, he said that he would kill himself if he left. I've lost a lot in my life, so I didn't want to be responsible for another life. I immediately told his mum who I suspect got him some help, but he hated me for telling her. Sometimes I wish that my parents had done more to protect and help me, so knowing that he had parents that would do anything for him gave me the ok to feel comfort in letting them know that he was struggling. Once I told my foster carer that we had broken up, she immediately thought I did something to muck it up. That hurt. I felt hurt that coerced me into having sex with me, but she didn't understand.

Moreover, I went into contact with my older sisters. Now that I wasn't in any contact with my dad or the family, I had hoped that I could talk to them. And I did. The oldest was still at university, studying graphic design whilst my other sister was studying English Literature and creative writing. I was in awe that they were doing something beautiful with their lives after everything that happened. Despite this, they were both in therapy, still dealing with the ordeal of what my dad put them through. It was a lot harder for my older sister to come to terms with my situation, as it only proved to her that my dad hadn't changed at all. I told them a bit about my younger sisters, but a sudden sadness came rushing over them as they now have other siblings they will never get to know. We met a few times in London, going to restaurants, visiting Camden market and even going to art exhibitions. The fact that I had them in my life felt so surreal. It was something that I dreamed of for nearly nine years. They were all grown up into these sophisticated women, and I hope my dad understands that he caused them a lot of pain. It made them stronger in some ways, and I was happy that I got to see them flourish in adulthood.

Seeing them get an education made me feel inspired. This is when I decided that I would put my life forward, especially with education. I was really good at English and loved writing. My English teacher saw a vast improvement in my writing, so I spent most hours working on that as well as my other subjects. She told me that I had a gift, and it was worth using. Many of the other students in my class struggled to write to the teacher's expectations; I used to be one of them kids. After our first mock exams of year eleven, I moved up in English into the top class. All of the other students in that class were really hard working, and I liked the thought of being challenged by my peers. My grades were gradually moving up, and this is when I wanted to start planning my future. I've always known that I like helping people, and since my education was becoming more stable, I was thinking of doing something in the academic route, such as teaching. It wouldn't have been without these amazing teachers in my life had I not wanted to think about a career. A quote that my foster mum always used to tell me was, "when you are ready to learn, the teacher will appear" which could apply to many different aspects of life. Determination and hard work are important, but so is the will to strive past barriers. I never thought in a million years that I could perform well in my studies, especially since I had moved around so much. I finally felt stable, just when I thought life and hope was done with me.

Unfortunately, during the time I was about to do my GCSEs, coronavirus hit the U.K and other countries around the globe. I was incredibly sad watching the news, hearing how many people were dying. I often wondered if my dad was one of those people, as many people with sickle cell died during this time too. We were told that any examinations would not take place, and so the grades released in the summer would be based on teacher predictions. Although I have always hated exams, I felt that I would not have the chance to release my full potential, which I am sure many others felt. My foster home had to adjust to this new situation, trying to keep everybody safe and sane at the same time. Lockdown allowed me to start writing my poetry again, this time with the thought of publishing it. I never finished it during this time, mainly because I was still dealing with the things that I wrote about. I was still having therapy during lockdown which helped my mental health a lot. We were talking more about my past, and other coping mechanisms that I could learn. The house was more chaotic than ever, with at least ten people in the home stuck together. To say we were driving each other mad was an understatement. All my foster sister wanted to do was leave. She begged my foster mum to let her go to her boyfriend's house for a couple of days, which was dangerous for obvious reasons. My foster mum protested that if she went, she wouldn't be able to come back because of the high-risk people in the home. I felt this was reasonable. My foster sister didn't.

The summer came and we started to spend more time in the garden. My foster parents opened the pool and we started to have barbeques. This was my favourite time, as we sat around the outside table just eating and talking. My foster father was building a fishpond during this time too, which turned out to be really beautiful. I enjoyed the walks in the garden as I have always found nature to be the most appealing thing on God's green earth. I used to sit in the garden writing in my diary about how I was doing, how life was progressing and how nervous I was to start my new chapter at sixth form. GCSE results day wasn't that far away, and so I was nervous about getting into the sixth form of my choice.

It arrived quite quickly, and I got my results in the email. My foster mother and I went on a walk before I got them, so I could clear my head and be calm once I received my results. I passed all of my GCSEs and got into the sixth form of my choice. No words could explain how proud I was. It was rare for me to be proud of myself, so the fact that I was meant to have achieved something worth celebrating. Later that day, I went into the sixth form to enrol. I spoke with the head of sixth form, as I didn't get quite what I needed to do history, but he still let me do it on a two-week trial basis. My foster family and I ordered a Chinese takeaway celebrating my achievements. I was incredibly happy at the thought of working towards something positive, so the fact that I did that made it feel even more special. That weekend, I went into London with my sisters to buy some clothes. They were also proud of me and how far I'd come, as I was now the third in line to go to sixth form. My parents never pursued their education later in life, and they never seemed to have any interest in my education either.

That September, I started sixth form. As I walked in the sixth form centre, I felt a wave of anxiety crush me. I was the new girl once again, only this time I was the second black girl in a room full of white people. I didn't talk to many people that day as it seemed that they were all really close with each other and had known one another since the start of secondary school. I made two friends at the start of the first term. One was a new girl who started at the same time as me and the other was a student who had been at the school since year seven. We shortly broke away and started to hang around other people. The first group that I joined were really friendly and welcomed me to sit with them. I liked hanging out with them until they started to exclude me out of things, I felt that I deserved better. A second lockdown hit again so I didn't have to talk to them if I didn't want to. I also made quite a few friends from my English class who thought I was nerdy because of my ideas of feminism. We had a group chat where we'd talk about the work assigned and anything else. I was beginning to feel more settled at the sixth form and found my place with the people I encountered.

Towards the end of year twelve, I started being invited to things. I went to a hippie theme party, hosted by one of the girls from my English class. I had lots of fun, and it was the first time I ever drank, but I didn't tell them that. My foster mum was surprised that I had a drink, mainly because she saw me as some golden child. Having my first drink didn't make me some sort of rebel, I actually felt that I was responsible and knew my limits. She still was shocked at my surprising behaviour to consume alcohol, which was reasonable, but sometimes I wish I could do the silly things that most seventeen year olds do. But even that sometimes came with a cost. The summer came and I went out as much as I could, exploring my life as a sixth former. A lot of the time I tried to fit in, but it was hard because these kids came from privileged backgrounds. I had worked harder than a lot of them, and sometimes I felt that they resented me for it.

I started year thirteen, the most challenging year I have ever experienced. I was applying to university while studying to get the grades I needed to get in, which felt like a lot of pressure. During this time, I met someone online. He was a lot older than me, so I didn't tell my foster mum. We met up secretly in London, where he took me on an uber boat. I'd never been on one of those before, so it was an experience I wanted to enjoy. We did this for a while, instead meeting in hotels. Although I enjoyed his company, it felt wrong. I had never been with an older guy before, so I felt like I needed to be mature, although I was in so many ways. It was going well for a while, until he told me that he contracted chlamydia. I was really upset, mainly because I trusted him enough to have unprotected intercourse, and also because he put my health at risk. He took me to a sexual health clinic where I had my blood taken, but because I was on my menstrual cycle, I couldn't do the full test. Although I appreciated everything that he did for me, I wasn't happy with being with someone who put myself and others at risk. He had a lot of unprotected sex, and I never really thought about it. In the meantime, I had to take antibiotics and was in regular contact with the sexual health team. Since I was inexperienced, I asked as many questions that I could about sexual diseases, contraception, fertility and other unimportant worries that I had. Once I got my blood results back, I got the all clear and decided that I would go on some contraception to protect myself from getting pregnant. I didn't want to be a teen mum for many reasons, but the main reason in particular was because I didn't want to end up like my mum. I wanted to work on my trauma, be financially stable, and emotionally available for my children. So I tried to be as careful as I could be for the foreseeable.

In November, I started to get sick. I had a fever for a couple of days and didn't understand why. When the weekend came, I was rushed into hospital, finding out that my appendix had abrupted and I needed to give them consent to do an operation. I was taken into the theatre room the same evening and operated on. The next day was really confusing for me. They took my appendix out, and said that they had other concerns, but I should take it up with the gp. I was annoyed that they didn't tell me because my mind became floating with the what-ifs. I had a go at the doctor for not treating me in the way I deserve, and then my foster mum reiterated my concerns once she came. I was discharged a day later, with the advice to rest for six weeks. I didn't. I went back to sixth form two weeks after so that I could find out my results of my mock exams I took before I got ill, and so that I can also catch up with the work that I missed. The sixth form team weren't exactly happy that I came back so quick against medical advice. I didn't care though, I was adamant to prove to myself that I can get the grades that I could work for, and so I did. In my first mock exam of year thirteen, I achieved an A* in English literature, and I could remember crying at the thought that I achieved something so high. I knew that there was a possibility that my grades would slightly drop after I came back, but I didn't really care because I knew of the impact I would face once I got ill.

After Christmas, things were looking better. Things went quite fast in terms of studying, balancing a social life and spending time with my foster family. I soon turned eighteen, which meant that my position in the family would change. I would no longer receive pocket money from social services, so I had to apply for universal credit to pay my foster mother turned host rent. I had a holiday job at the time, so I had a little money for myself every now and then. I could see a change in the relationship between me and my foster mother, which made me feel quite lonely. I went back online to search for love, which I did for a short time. I met a boy who lived in the West Midlands. We talked quite a bit on the phone when I wasn't studying and planned to meet in the Easter holidays before my exams. I met his mum and sister, who were the kindest, but never met his dad. He told me that he used to beat his family, which led to his mum running away taking him and his sister far away. I saw the sadness of the thought of talking about this did to him, so we never talked about it again.

Shortly after I began my relationship with him, I found out I was pregnant. I was overwhelmed with panic, but mostly joy. It gave me a new hope; I had someone to love and care for and also to protect.

For some reason I wanted to do all of those things. I never told anyone about my pregnancy because a part of me was embarrassed. How would I explain that I got pregnant by a boy that I've only known for a short amount of time? Nonetheless, I told him. He was upset because he thought that the baby would ruin my life. I disagreed. Something that I remember someone told me was that there was no better gift than life. I wanted to be the mother that my mother never was. So I ended things with him, determined that I could do this on my own. I got a more stabilised job to start bringing in some income so that I could save for the baby, and maybe get a place somewhere else. I was still doing my A-levels during this time, which needless to say was another thing to worry about, but I was determined to do it all. Unfortunately, all the hope and plans didn't last long. One morning, I woke up in a pool in my own blood, and I already knew what happened. I lost my baby. I couldn't believe it. The moment of being pregnant felt too good to be true. I know it might not have been my time, but I so badly wanted it to be.

I couldn't deal with the loss, it was too much to handle. The fact that I had to keep it a secret made it even harder to grieve. So once again, I attempted another suicide. I overdosed on my antidepressants in my bedroom. My foster mum found me and was confused as to why I would do this to myself after all this time. I just told her that I was struggling, I didn't want her to know about my tragic loss. After my overdose I was admitted to hospital where I had to take part of a program to take time out to figure out what has happened and how I would move forward. The mental health team encouraged me to take my A-levels, go to university and work on my coping mechanism skills. I didn't want to take my exams after everything that happened, especially since I only had a week left to get my head in the game. I accepted that I needed to do this for myself, and my angel up in heaven. I worked hard within the last week, hoping that I would still do well enough to get into university. It's crazy how many hurdles life can throw at you and still manage to get up on your feet and carry on.

My A-level exams went quickly, but whenever I had free time, I thought about my angel. I was glad that nobody could clip her wings, that she could fly in the sky and blossom without the weight of the world on her shoulders. I imagined she was a girl, my beautiful glowing skin with her father's ocean blue eyes. She was going to be loved unconditionally and she would have known it, because there wouldn't be a day where I wouldn't have told her and showed her. Once A-levels were over, I started counselling to start my grieving process. I told the counsellor everything, but mainly about how I hadn't had time to process my grief. She suggested going to a grave where babies were buried, but I never went. My baby wasn't developed enough to even be buried, so all I have to remember her is the bloody bed sheets that I washed straight away so that nobody in the house would suspect anything. I just felt crushed by the fact I wasn't even able to carry until the end of my first trimester. I felt like a failure in so many ways. I was deeply disappointed. Now, I understand that some things happen for a reason, and one day I will have a beautiful family and a loving husband, and then it will finally be my time for things to fall in place.

Part Four

*T*he summer came, and I decided to rest and enjoy the time that I have before university. I went to the Isle of Wight with four of my friends. We had our own house and we stayed there for a week. We went on walks, went into the town and got new piercings with my friend. I guess you could say that I went piercing crazy in the summer, despite the little money I had for the week. We'd cook lots together, watch anime and play card games at the dining table. We visited a few beaches and I embraced the cold wind on my face and loved the feeling of standing on the rocks. I felt at peace, enjoying the small things of life. By the end of the week, one of my friends went home as her boyfriend broke up with her, so her parents picked her up in Portsmouth near the ferry. It was sad, and she was missed, but it also made me wonder what it is like to feel sad when you lose someone you romantically love, as it never bothered me when I broke up with the people I dated. I started to talk to somebody again, and he was older than any of the guys I dated. He seemed fun and crazy, and I felt that I deserved the break from all the seriousness of life.

When we came back, prom was the next day. I brought a gown that complimented my eyes and skin. I did my makeup, and my foster sister did my lashes. I was ready to have the last experience of sixth form, saying my temporary goodbye until results day. People got rewards for their interesting personalities; we were offered champagne and had a professional photographer capture this wonderful moment. Afterwards I went to an after party and got black out drunk. I lost my phone so I couldn't contact my foster mother. I began to get anxious because I knew she'd get mad. My friend's mum dropped me home, and as expected, she was mad. She thought I lost my phone on purpose, which I didn't, but she didn't believe me anyway. I went to bed with tears rolling down my face. I felt that I ruined everything. The next day I packed a bag, telling her I went to a friends for a couple of days to get some space. But I didn't. Something inside my hurt soul sent me to my mum's unexpectedly. I knocked and she answered. It felt weird, calling for home where my heart doesn't belong. I asked her if I could stay for a couple of days and she let me.

It was awkward at the start, mainly because I hadn't seen her in almost seven years. She was married now, and my brother could talk, walk, and throw the largest tantrum I'd ever seen. My older brother came to stay with us whilst I was there to see me. He didn't live there anymore because he also found things difficult with mum. I didn't know that, and part of me felt that I left him behind when I wasn't the only one that was struggling. I spent some time with my younger brother and had the best time. He was careless, young and free, and so I was happy that my mum gave him this life. During the time I was in London, I met up with the boy I was talking to. We had dinner and wine, which turned into sex. I didn't feel null and void about it, I just felt free. I made the decision to choose whatever happiness I wanted, and so I did that. By the end of the week, I decided that I needed to talk to my foster mum and lay everything out on the table.

I told her about my miscarriage, the boys I met online, and the struggles of my studies. She paused quite a few times, like she didn't know what to say. She asked me when all of this happened, and so I told her. I never meant for her to lose trust in me, but I was also losing trust in myself. I didn't know how to make myself happy anymore, and so I chased those who were so willing to give it to me. I knew that she saw me in a different light, but it is something that I had to accept. I was changing, and I also needed to adjust to that. Over the summer I went to see my mum more. She invited me to her graduation, where she gained a degree in psychology and sociology. I was so proud. She was finally chasing her dreams, and I was glad to have the front row seat watching this.

The guy I was seeing made me his girlfriend, and I was happy. The relationship after a while became very toxic, making each time harder to leave. I didn't want love to be painful anymore, yet it was the only love I thought I deserved. One evening on my mum's birthday, we had an argument at his place. My mum invited him to celebrate her birthday, but I didn't want him to come. I had explained this, but instead of a conversation it turned into a heated argument, leading to him putting his hands on me. I was instantly terrified. All I wanted to do was to leave the room at that moment, but he didn't want me to leave because he thought I was going to tell the police. He took my phone and then left the room for a bit. I found my phone and ran out of the room as fast as I could. I tried to call anyone that I could, but no answer. I just cried in a park near his house, wishing that my life would stop involving such pain and suffering. After an hour, I went back to my mum's place and told her that we had broken up. She seemed sad. I didn't know whether she was sad for me or sad that she could no longer replace the muck up she called my brother. The next day she took me to my aunt's house in Harrow, where we ate cake and caught up on my life. I told her that I got into university and had just finished my A-levels. She didn't know that I was in care for the years that she hadn't seen me, because my mum told her I was living with my dad. It seemed as if she was embarrassed of my struggles, but I only struggled because she started my struggle. Nonetheless, I had a good time that day, then went home back to my foster mother's the next day.

My foster mother and I started to make plans for what I needed to buy for university. We had a day of shopping, buying essentials for the kitchen and bathroom, and decorations for my bedroom. It was a nice distraction but also it helped put things into perspective. I had a few days before I was about to move to university, and I was getting more excited. The day finally came, and I woke up at six o'clock as we were hitting the road early. I slept the whole way there, and when we finally arrived it was like I jumped into a different universe. I was one of the first people to arrive, then later met who would be my flatmates. We talked about where we lived, and the sort of A-levels we picked. I went onto the campus to enrol for the academic year, and talked to financial advisors about the bursaries I was entitled to. I decorated my room first, giving it an artsy look with fake leaves on the ceiling, an art canvas on the wall, and my stationery to sit on the desk. I wanted to make it feel as home as possible, because this was now my new home. They had parties on campus throughout the week, known as freshers' week. I met quite a few people there, introducing myself and also getting to know them whilst drunk. I also met someone special who I have in my life, even at this current moment. We met at a club in town where all the local students go to. He told one of my new friends that I was pretty. The rest became history.

The first couple of months I really struggled with my mental health. It was worse than ever. I felt isolated and stopped attending my classes for a while. I didn't bother to make friends anymore, and just wanted to be alone in the dark. I decided to get some help and my boyfriend supported me with this. He came to every hospital appointment, every counselling appointment, and everything in between. The time we spent together made it easier to feel some sort of happiness, but deep down I wasn't happy with myself. I wanted to put the work in so I could credit myself, not say that it was my boyfriend that lifted me out of the darkness. I took on meditation and started a new antidepressant, alongside going to the gym every once in a while. I also tried to socialise when I felt up for it, but battling against my mental health became a challenge I wasn't ready for.

The holidays came, and I decided I would stay with my mum for the meantime. I met up with my boyfriend to see his family to watch the world cup with them and had the most amazing time. His family are from Argentina and have very strong cultural ties, and I loved that about them. Despite living in the UK for nineteen years, they brought Argentina to their household. It was mesmerising to witness. When I went home, my mum was being extremely difficult. She always wanted to go off somewhere, leaving me with my little brother. I layed it down to her that this was not acceptable, and her first priorities should be her children. She snapped and immediately triggered me, so I left. My boyfriend's family said I could stay with them for the meantime, but I was so far deep into my depression pit that I didn't want to burden them. I returned to university halls, where I attempted my suicide. The ambulance was called by the university who came to check up on me, and my boyfriend immediately came from London to see me in hospital. I discharged myself the next day and went back to his. We spent Christmas day together; his mum made me a salmon wellington and we opened gifts together. He gave me the family I always wanted, and so I will always be grateful for that.

The New Year came, and I wanted to start it out with a bang. I started writing this book you are currently reading. I decided to take some control of my life and show you that it is possible to find hope in the lost stars. I hurt every day. I am not always happy. But one thing I can tell you is that I never stop trying. I get up on days where I don't feel like it, and I keep going. I believe you can too, and I hope this book brings you comfort.

Lightning Source UK Ltd.
Milton Keynes UK
UKHW011903020323
417942UK00001B/25